truth
love
and
the lines
in   between

poems by

Paul Rabinowitz

Finishing Line Press
Georgetown, Kentucky

truth
   love
and
   the lines
in   between

Copyright © 2023 by Paul Rabinowitz
ISBN 979-8-88838-307-0 First Edition
All rights reserved under International and Pan-American Copyright Conventions. No part of this book may be reproduced in any manner whatsoever without written permission from the publisher, except in the case of brief quotations embodied in critical articles and reviews.

ACKNOWLEDGMENTS

I would like to thank these magazines, journals and presses for giving homes to versions of the poems in this manuscript:"Spin Cycle," "Softcover," "Rose": *The Montreal Review*; "Indigo and Half Moon": *The Writing Disorder*; "The Wish": *Metaworker Literary Journal*; "Citrus Honey Cake," "Vacations": *Evening Street Press*; "Speeding Ticket": *Grey Sparrow Journal*; "Tongue Tied" (originally appeared as "Shirtless)," "Indigo": *The Oddville Press*; "Dolly": *The Courtship of Winds*; "Global Warming": *New World Writing*; "The Monastery": *Adirondack Review*; "The Cat": *Authors and Artists Anthology*; "Slackwater" (originally appeared as "Soundscape"): *Authors and Artists Anthology*; "Nightstand": *The Bangalore Review*; "Self Portrait as Woman With Scarf": *The Metaworker*; "Villa Dei Misteri": *Pif Magazine*,"In The Original Language": *The Zodiac Review*; "Supernovas," "Quiet Mornings," "Temporary Exhibit": *Wilderness House Literary Review*.

I owe much gratitude to the literary journals that printed my words. Also to the artists who offered encouragement and collaborated with me on the films and performances inspired by these poems. In particular, Kathy Kremins, Jessy Brodsky, Georgia Usborne, Elaina Stewart, Amit Weiner, Kathleen Kelley, Oksana Horban, AJ Tasley Parr, Marsha Pierre Guirlande and Maxine Steinman, all with me as I navigated the art museums of the world and explored the lines in between.

Publisher: Leah Huete de Maines
Editor: Christen Kincaid
Cover Art: Paul Rabinowitz
Author Photo: Megan Rabinowitz
Cover Design: Sydney Prusso

Order online: www.finishinglinepress.com
also available on amazon.com

Author inquiries and mail orders:
Finishing Line Press
P. O. Box 1626
Georgetown, Kentucky 40324
U. S. A.

Table of Contents

Summer

Spin Cycle 1
Moon Illuminating Dark Features 2
In The Original Language 3
Speeding Ticket 5
Global Warming 6
Dolly 7
Tongue Tied 8
Scotoma 9
Grand St., Revisited 10
Citrus Honey Cake 12
Quiet Morning 13
Supernovas 14

Fall

The Forbidden Apple 17
Nightstand 18
Temporary Exhibit 21
Self Portrait as Woman with Scarf 22
Slack Water 24
The Wish 25
Words That Come To Mind When You Come To Mind ... 26
Another Late Night With My Writing Group 27
Bare Trees 28
Indigo and Half Moon 30

Winter

Softcover 39
Revising 40
Us Writers 41
Mild Brie With Red Bordeaux 42
Confessional 44
Storm of the Century 45

Lies 46
Cold Snap 47
Secret Life of Voice 48
Woman Selling Flowers at the Lorimer Stop 49

Spring

Villa Dei Misteri 53
4 Syllables 55
Betrayal 56
Vacations 57
Electric Massager 58
The Mechanics of Photography 59
The Cat 60
Rose 62
Too Much Emphasis On My Needs 63
The Monastery 64
A.D.D. 65
Do Not Disturb 67
My Last Poem in a Series 68
Blood Red Morning 69
The Lines In Between 70

The poems and stories you are about to encounter are wrapped up in the journey of a person at the beginning of his second act. At 50 years old I took a day off from my routine and traveled from my suburban home to an open door somewhere near Grand Street in Williamsburg, Brooklyn. I found art. Ten years later, I exited through the back holding photographs, films and stories about truth, love and the lines in between.

This collection is dedicated to people who never give up searching for what might lie on the other side. We have no specific reason for why we do this. It's not for fame or to increase our nest egg, rather we are drawn to sparks that can ignite inner flames. We have this insatiable desire to get closer to some kind of truth even if we have to crawl through mud to get there. In the end the best I can hope for is to learn a bit more about myself or why I ended up in an industrial section of Greenpoint, Brooklyn next to the Sanitation Department's *silver eggs* sewage treatment plant reading a prose piece about longing. Or how I landed at Karloff's, a Belorussian bar in Carroll Gardens to read poems about Hurricane Katrina at an open mic in front of a mostly Russian speaking audience. Perhaps I missed some things in the first act, or need to rethink my place on stage before the second half comes to a close. Or more simply, it might be etched upon my DNA. All this is still unclear to me but one thing is certain—at the final bow there will be a voice in the audience yelling something from her seat. The echo will sound like *curiosity*. The person will be wearing a yellow dress.

"He wanted to learn more about himself," she'll whisper to her friend sitting next to her. "Step closer to the truth."

"How do you know?"

"When I first met him he was leaning over a rail at the end of a pier under a dimming light. When he heard footsteps he turned. I heard him say something about drifting. How one's soul can crash like an endless sea. Then bent down on one knee, removed a journal from his backpack and started writing

one line
    then another
a foghorn
    in the distance
wails

Summer

July 14

Spin Cycle

I remember
the first time

a hot summer day
   Angels Laundromat

waiting for stains
to be released
from the fibers
of my white
collared shirt

across the folding table
your
       sparkling eyes

a tarnished
gold band
I slide from
my finger

as you remove
your clothes
from a wicker basket

ask if I can spare
detergent

turn the knob to
        heavy-load

and watch suds
bust 'round
your yellow dress

water darkening
with each churn

July 21

Moon Illuminating Dark Features

I want to leave in the line about the
moon illuminating your dark features
because the language is bold
flows off my tongue like water

but when I looked up
only a thin sliver
of waxing crescent appeared

and without my glasses
not even sure it was you

July 25

In the Original Language

I understand what Adam went through in the garden in July on the first day when all was calm and the wind barely blew as things were slowly being figured out but wonder what Eve was looking for because she understood more than he would ever know and she was complete and her body was truth and like a dancer that moves away from a small town in Ohio or New Mexico or a place that no one goes to unless someone is dying you found me sitting alone on a park bench with paper and pen and said your name in the original which is Chaya as in living as in the present tense and I thought who would name their child living unless they believed she will continue dancing despite the tragic end of the first act as in the way your body springs as you walk across the grass with strong torso extended neck and ballet slippers dangling from ribbons strewn over wide shoulders and I deliberate about the enormity of our next move together but like a visionary you've already choreographed in your mind how this will all play out on stage as your eyes scan this perfect space of fruits and flowers even a stream tumbling through a crack in the rock down a cliff into a small pool where two gazelles gather drinking fresh water and you look at me with those gentle eyes knowing I lack experience unsure if I can do any of this here with you in July then like the sweet sound of chirping crickets I hear three words that sound like

I know you

blending with the gurgling pulse of water over smooth rocks and turn my head towards the crevice of your mouth to make sure I understand the words in the original language and realize I have never heard a dancer speak while on stage

If this is part of the living performance then how should I take these three words that cause my body to tremble and wonder if you are aware of how words can trigger something this new world has never felt

I am still learning

and succumb to this moment knowing the three words you speak are now living inside me and the wild garden you have chosen for this act is within you as you are knowing but I am still gathering and wonder how will others know about this moment and will they question the act so do I need to record this or should the act of living be all we need? what of those who don't understand the words in the original? so I pull a piece of dry grass from the field reach for low hanging fruit then squeeze the juice into your palm dip the reed into the ink onto your perfect body and write Adam then next to it the word Desire and with the tip of the reed dripping red I scribe your name in the present tense in the original language and feel my pulsating body contract as you smile with each stroke of the reed then you ask me to write a poem about a dancer and turn towards me exposing your thighs my hand moving like the gazelle skipping over rocks and I look around at this setting the reed on your flesh and the words flow out from my body in the original language we spoke together for the first time on a perfect day in July in the garden and I question if this is living then will I stay here with you forever or until something in the new world that we can not explain turns

and the weather cools

rain pours down hard from the dark sky above and with no protection our bodies shiver and the living words written in the original language across your body wash off and I wonder

if living is changing and knowing is forgetting

so when the scenes of the perfect garden fade I return to Ohio or New Mexico or someplace where names are in past tense and the original is sin

I turn to look at you for the last time knowing I might never see anything like this again

July 30

Speeding Ticket

Ode to my speeding ticket
proving that a man my age can still be reckless
and do what he wants when he feels like it
without any care of consequence

flashing me back to the days of rebellious youth
when I dropped my first hit of acid with my best friend
at his parent's formal dinner party

told my girlfriend I'll go there if she goes there
and without any thought risked a year in military prison
threatening the captain who put my brothers at too much risk

Now with this speeding ticket I wait 'till the last day permitted
without penalty to send my check
placing the stamp horizontal

August 2

Global Warming

I'm trying to find out how you feel about me before the warming of the globe causes seas to rise and floods the small coastal town I've called home for 30 years and turbulent waters smash seawalls and inundate basements causing mold and mildew and a state of emergency is declared and you can no longer get to me and I am alone with pump in hand purchased when I knew I needed to know how you feel about me and wanted to live a long life and see you often like one looks at the night sky and marvels at the stars and all the distant light in the universe when there is no moon or clouds or threat of rain and maybe with the help of this apparatus I can live a long life or at least one more day and not be drowned by a catastrophe brought about by rapid changes in temperature and I struggle with this more than you can imagine and think about you more than you know and wake in the middle of the night soaked in sweat by a recurring dream that I die before I know how you feel about me and with eyes half closed I stumble down the stairs to turn on the television to check the weather to be sure there is no chance of rain in the near future or at least for tomorrow and stay awake until morning sucks the remaining life from me and walk around dead like wondering how you feel about me until it becomes all too much and one day I pack a suitcase and leave my coastal town that I've lived in for 30 years and find a new place on a hill that is dry and far from potential floods and set roots in a stone house far away from anything familiar and start to breath normal again and rise fresh each morning after dreamless nights and walk outside in the bright sunlight and marvel at the cloudless sky with no threat of rain and inhale the wild scent of thyme and rosemary and the thought of storms or flooding or even the way you feel about me never crosses my mind and I return to the stone cottage excited for the day and sit at my desk and begin to write a new story about a man who moves to Jerusalem and lives on a hill overlooking the desert where it never rains and summer heat is dry and oppressive and everything turns brown and dies from lack of water except for the wild thyme and rosemary that is fragrant and everywhere and all this is new to the man who moved here to be alone and distant from anything in his memory and far from everything in his past and for some reason I can not explain in the middle of all this I open the daily paper and read about a bomb on a bus and underneath the photo of the catastrophe and ensuing firestorm in small print is a story about one of the victims from a small coastal town who was coming to Jerusalem for the first time to surprise a friend and I close the paper and walk out of my cottage that is high on a hill in the city of sadness and wonder when the rains might come and wash the dust from all these stones.

August 9

Dolly

I had the most interesting dream last night
about a woman who dressed like Salvador Dali
and a man who dressed like his muse, Gala

Each impression of the other fell for the impression
of the other but when their true selves were revealed
the man who dressed as Gala decided to borrow
the clothes from the woman who dressed as Dali

The woman was so moved, she dressed in the clothes
of his muse Gala, and together they decided to photograph
each other with an old camera that had no film, yet the idea
of the photo that never came to be became the idea for a novel
that was never written as he removed his tie
setting it on the waxed end of her elegant mustache.

August 15

Tongue Tied

It would be easy to explain
if I were shirtless,
covered in paint

atop a twelve
foot ladder
layers of drop cloth
underneath

Beethoven's concerto
number five blaring,

with brush in hand,
muscles flexed,
I lean into a canvas

applying final touches
around corners
of your mouth.

But instead, I sit alone
with small fingers
on plastic keys

conjuring stories
about a conflicted artist
who paints scenes of longing

in early dawn
waiting for drips of light,
to uncover his darkness.

August 18

Scotoma

Maybe I should try
color film
the next time
I photograph you

so others
will see
why I choose
black and white

minimizing retina damage
like staring
at the sun
without protection

August 25

Grand Street, Revisited

a song
bird
clutches
a thin
branch
on Grand
Street

a familiar
tune,
echoing
memories
of
spring

I stop
and
listen,
notice
a woman
through
lace
curtains

Dylan's Blonde on
Blonde,
pinned
to the wall

her spine
curved
like
in prayer

half her
face
elusive,

lost in
shadow
the other,
yearning
or hiding
something

and
wonder
can trills,
and non
existent
pauses
from song
birds,
over time

ultimately
penetrate
brick

September 2

Citrus Honey Cake

I don't have a fancy name or moniker
no one calls me Spirit Child
only what my father gave me,
and what his father gave him

Once I asked my grandfather
if he ever listened to Brian Wilson's arrangements on Pet Sounds
or watched the setting sun from a sandy beach

"Only a rich man has time for that," he said

I recall a story he told my father, about a customer
who sang in the night club across from his tailor shop

The way her voice transported him to springtime in the old country
How he wished he had the words to tell her all this in English

Instead he offered her a cup of his fresh brewed Romanian coffee
And cut an extra large slice of citrus honey cake he made from scratch

September 6

Quiet Morning

If I were a true poet
I wouldn't sit for hours
with curved spine
and hunched back
laboring over every word
wondering how it might sound
when read in the stillness
of your quiet morning

Instead I'd put down
my pen, extend my hand
and wait for music
of the milonga
to swirl between us
your dark eyes
surrendering
to my cabeceo

September 16

Supernovas

I've grown tired of the way your eyes
flash when the setting sun dips below
the wide brim of your fedora

translucent like a yellow moon
over orange sandstone floating high
above the desert floor, Venus

brighter than a million stars
in a distant galaxy with black holes
supernovas exploding then dying
and exploding again

drained from it all I put down my pen

shut my eyes but hear a ringing
like church bells, your voice
rising then swirling and rising again
shaking my body
lifting me to higher ground

Fall

September 29

The Forbidden Apple

I wonder if the writer who penned the phrase

    truth

        sets

            you

                free

ever tried conjuring a poem
while eating strawberries
picked fresh from your garden
while your cat swipes at my hand
and you say

he does that to anyone
who lingers too long
gazing into my eyes
sitting in his spot
thinking about forbidden fruit

September 30

Nightstand

These days
I only read works
from poets
I'm intimate with

not the cigarette
afterwards kind
but more
in a crowded
room kind

when you read
that piece
about smoking
a cigarette
afterwards

lips pursed
'round a narrow
filter inhaling
nicotine
your body
absorbing poison

eyes shift
to a copy of
Gideon's Bible
on the nightstand
next to a stained
panel wall

thoughts drift
to another place
like a crowded
room with
adoring fans

clapping
and snapping
and you forget
to tap the ash
so it tumbles
onto linen
burning small holes

I push past
the audience
with heart racing
purchase
the last copy

ask you
to sign your name
and place it
on my nightstand
next to an ashtray

I took from
an old motel
I stopped into
one night

after working
late somewhere
near Bayonne
and open
the book
to that poem

inhale the fragrance
lingering
from your fingers

where you signed
your name
under the title

on a clear
white page

next to a graphic
of a long ash
across a bible
on a nightstand
still burning

October 2

Temporary Exhibit

Why is it when I visit
the great art museums
all I do is watch the curious

necks elongated
teeth clamped on lips
eyes like slits
maybe staring at a Picasso

and when they turn
to look at me
studying them
I feel overwhelmed

these patrons of great art
would take a moment
to analyze
what's in front of them

in the flesh
curved spine
against blank
white wall

inside the greatest
art museum
in the world

October 4
Self Portrait as Woman with Scarf

I have no hair atop my head but if I did it would be like yours and I'd wash it brush it out and take care of it and on occasion part it to one side and work it into a low rolled bun or sleek ponytail or maybe even a twisted crown flower braid depending on how I feel in the morning and you'd glance at it and marvel at me and my creativity and when we would be waiting in line together during our brief encounters in the morning when our paths cross on our way to work ordering the usual cappuccinos I could say something coy to the barista and watch your lips stretch across white teeth and a tingle would dance up my spine and I would experience a moment of weightlessness when your wide eyes would linger a top my head marveling at the loose bun I crafted this morning like the premier dancer at the Joffrey Ballet and you could gather ideas for your next poem and I would lean my head back and run my hands over the smooth part at the crown or slip my fingertips into the twisted mass and like a gentle wave touching the shoreline the strands would roll down past my shoulders and spread out over my bare arms until a picture is etched in your memory

    Knowing this I would gather my hair and twist it then place it all to one side exposing my neck in such a way that you would want to press your face into the long curve inhale the sweet scent of conditioner and remain there for a moment and would not smell the cigarette smoke your husband blew into your face this morning because you were feeling inspired typing a new poem in a style that was different to anything you had tried before but he wanted breakfast before going to work
Your fingers moved quickly to finish and smiled occasionally at the screen ignoring his voice which you had learned to fear when he was tired of waiting and pleaded with him for just another minute to finish the last line so as not to forget the vision of what brought you there in the first place—the cover of a book I showed you last week at the cafe during our usual brief encounter—Frida Kahlo in a chair in her lover's clothes tufts of black hair strewn over a dark wood floor
He wanted breakfast and you continued typing not so much in defiance but because at that moment you were closing in on some sort of truth that could bring you to the point where you could remove everything that is dear to you
And told me that morning you felt a tingling on your scalp and glanced at yourself in the mirror after finishing your new poem and reading through it again to be sure the line breaks made sense then he turned and heaved his coffee cup across the room glass shattered everywhere but you did not look up from your edits as he stepped over the shards and walked out and you closed

the cover of your laptop grabbed scissors from the drawer and said to me that when it was all done you experienced a moment of weightlessness

swept the remains into a pile and gathered it into a large box because that is how much you had and tied a ribbon around it left the keys next to the box and walked out to the usual cafe where we met for our brief encounters in the morning and you ordered not your usual cappuccino with cinnamon but a dark roast

And before going our separate ways to our jobs I did as I did so many times before and waited for you to let your hair down and twist it and you would say something that made me laugh and I would absorb your words that stay with me until the next time but today you wear a scarf and I offer to pay for your dark roast and notice your eyes welling up so I hand you a napkin and say something coy then watch as your lips stretch across your white teeth the color returns to your face and you extend your hands gently touching my bare head

October 6

Slack Water

After making coffee
much the
same way
every morning
I cover my head
with favorite hoodie
click on
ocean wave
soundscape
and prepare
for the act
of another
little love poem
but nothing

              except   images

 seagulls   distant shores

and recall
the first time

vinyl slips
through
weathered
sleeve
cotton dress
unfurling

Tom Waits
spinning
on your player
something about
Ahab and drifting

October 8

The Wish

What if I could
paint like you
piercing light through
darkening skies

if I could weave stories
by blending chapters
about love and discontent

what if I stood naked
sang love songs
that pry hearts open
like the edge
of a knife

I wouldn't struggle
with the truth

no need for crayons
whose tips are flat
from making rainbows

I could delete
my tired sentences
with dubious
meanings

be free of burden

then
perhaps
you would look
at me

October 19
Words That Come to Mind When You Come to Mind

Maybe,
        incandescent
is closer
to the truth

November 8

Another Late Night With My Writing Group

This morning
with eyes
blurred
from last night's
Bordeaux

I sit at my computer
trying to remember
the edits
you suggested
for my cat poems

but when
my brain
finally triggers
impulses
to my fingers

the only letters
they land
upon are
        Y
                     O
            U

November 15

Bare Trees

I never understood what all the talk was about
when they brought up
renewal
another cycle of seasons
eternal hope

I'm not even sure who they are
but kept asking
believing
one day
it might happen
like a seed
pushing through
frozen ground
or a pedal
after morning rain
unfolding

so today
I wake early
chose a pair of jeans
brown boots
wool cap,
worn leather jacket
as if today
might be the day

   and step out
sidewalks lined
with bare trees
fallen leaves

hear tapping
on the pavement
glance up
at your brown boots
jeans, snug leather jacket
wool cap

and in passing
hear you whisper
something
like

don't listen
to their lies
about spring
renewal
cycle of seasons

hold on
to your promise
'cause in the end
all you'll have
is this moment
to live and relive
over and over

until winter
blankets the street
summer
cracks the pavement
and you'll
read them a poem
about the first time
in autumn

wool caps
leather jackets
and no eternal hope
for anything
except
fleeting moments
that remain
with you
forever

November 23

Indigo and Half Moon

11:46 a.m.

A woman wearing a down jacket with silver duct tape clutches the hand of a young child. She throws a half empty coffee cup into the bin under the counter, walks past a full length mirror and glances at her reflection. Twisting her torso to fit into the frame she piles her hair atop her head and notices a gentleman in the back of the cafe gazing at her. She turns towards the exit then cranes her neck to check storm clouds gathering over a playground at the intersection of Pitt and Grand Street. She hoists the child and steps out. Moments later they return. She hushes the crying child that clutches her soaked jacket. The gentleman in the corner of the crowded cafe signals to them to take a seat at the table where he sits. She glances at me sketching the scene then releases her wet hair. I watch as it falls around her shoulders. She sets the child down as the gentleman rises, waving to get her attention. The woman saunters across the floor like a prima donna on stage. He reaches into his worn travel bag and gives the mother a bright blue bird. She rubs her hand over the soft fabric. The child grabs the stuffed animal and runs to the mirror. Glancing at her reflection, she sways back and forth with two hands clutching the wings. She catches my gaze and freezes. The mother turns away from her daughter's reflection, pushes a candle jar to the edge and leans across the table close to the gentleman. She remains focused on the movement of his lips. The child stomps her feet, puts the bird under her jacket then disappears among the crowds gathering on Grand Street

2:53 p.m.

If I use
a phrase
like
bird enthusiast
with
blue eyes
gentle
voice

in the
first stanza
of my poem

will I need
anything
else
for the middle
or end

to explain
why you
grab

star chart
and dream catcher
earrings

and meet
a bird watcher

to view
a male
bunting

perched
atop
a cactus
singing
to stake
its claim

plumage
brilliant
and shiny
illuminated
under
indigo
sky

waiting
patiently
for nightfall
star patterns
to appear

for clues

to navigate
a vast
intoxicating
desert

while
half moon
in the distance
rises

4:43 p.m.

In a state
of hypnotic
hyper-focused
confusion
a moth
hovers
near a chosen
candle

thinking
the flame
is the moon
glowing
the nocturnal
creature
rises
then falls
unable to

break
its evolutionary
navigational
system

as when you
limp
past the mirror
check
storm clouds
eyes glazed
like a boxer
hit on the jaw

neck snaps
light dims
while falling
to the ground
wishing
someone
laid a pillow
on the canvas

and in a state
of hypnotic
hyper-focused
confusion
you twist
your head
glance at me
sketching
the scene
throwing fresh
words
on my paper
like a painter
under night sky
full moon
igniting

desert
landscapes

as you rise

order coffee
extra cream
and sugar
find a cushioned
chair
to rest upon
until storm clouds
break

I slide
my poem
across the table
revealing
colorful phrases like

new places
we'll travel to

sand soaked
in orange light

eternal summers
with no past

break the chain
around your neck

like Jackson Pollock
day after day
I'll splash
new words
against adobe
walls
indigo dripping

over
raw sienna

so when your offspring
returns
finds us
burning
from both ends
we'll watch
as she throws
the animal
into the air

and wait
to see
which direction
the dry wind
blows

where
the bird
lands

Winter

December 22

Softcover

I open
the blinds
cursing

biting cold
slashes flesh
our cottage
not made
for winter

Outside
a red-tailed hawk
pins
a hare
under talons

carnage
litters
the virgin snow

Inside
spread open
upon your pillow
a book
with soft cover

a love story
of sorts

the kind
I never read

December 29

Revising

Still revising myself into an eagle
circling over a frozen river above
Narrowsburg New York watching
you lean over a rickety balcony in
winter coat outside The Heron Cafe
hair whipping across your face
taking photos of my wingspan

concrete falling from rusty beams
you appear miniature one eye
pressed against viewfinder finger
hovering over metal button with
talons open I swoop in close sensing
heart palpitations under heavy coat
hear a sound in the wind like *beautiful*

throwing me slightly off balance
like when you suggested revising
my story into a poem from the heart
as you press on the button step back
roll up your fur collar against bare neck
shielding any attempt to taste flesh

then land on an unsuspecting hare
the last stanza of my poem oozing onto
solid ice as you secure the lens cap
return to the warm glow of the cafe
your main course laid out before you

soaring east far from the frozen river
to complete revisions started when I first
saw you in open field camera in hand
kneeling above an injured bird shadows
cut across your neck like ceiling fan blades
turkey vultures circling overhead

January 23

Us Writers

I remember it was Bernie
who penned this song for Elton
alone in his room
on a rainy morning
not because he needed something more
to live on than black coffee
or cheap wine
nor did he ever think
about life with a top 10 hit

just because us writers have this thing

So when I see your eyes darting
from this poem to the unpaid bills
I am comforted to know
in 50 years no one will remember
it was I who penned this poem for you
but will see only a legend
with studded jacket
rhinestone glasses and a wig
so large it buried his head

February 5

Mild Brie with Red Bordeaux

Sometimes
when reading
my poems
on stage
in front
of an audience
I struggle
to remember
how I got there

then glance
over at the bar
see your face
half alight
and wonder why
anyone might choose
to give up
an evening
at home
savoring a bordeaux
with mild brie
hearth glowing
face half alight
looking out the window
for footprints
under street lamps
pressed in fresh snow

so I adjust my glasses
grasp the mic stand
and like a street map
unfold my latest poem
lines crossing
leading me
to an empty stool
at the bar
salty chip scraps

scattered next to
peeled beer bottle labels

ask the audience
for forgiveness
as I step out
trace the route
back to a street lamp
roaring fire
mild brie with
red bordeaux
in one hand
the microphone
off switch
in the other

February 9

Confessional

Last night
I tried
editing my
confessional
but couldn't
figure
where
to put
the period

February 12

Storm of the Century

Since you left
a cold silence
pervades
the room

ticking clocks
penetrate walls
while snowflakes
sculpt the landscape

I remember
you said
they're predicting
the storm of the century

as dusk
blankets the day
tocks fade
to a whimper

mounds of snow
cause residential streets
to be deemed
impassable

February 15

Lies

I prefer Tom Waits
over truth

February 24

Cold Snap

Walking with you
in the dead of winter
trees exploding in the vacant air
you said even drops of sap
have water and can freeze suddenly
one by one like gunshots

March 2

Secret Life of Voice

The phrasing
in my latest poem
seems flat
so I tap my back arrow key
in 4/4 time
delete the existing stanza
close my eyes
and type

songs in the key of life

your hips rolling
as you pull the album
from the collection
needle on vinyl
heart pounds
like rising notes
only the sound
of your voice
guiding these
waking fingers

March 9

Woman Selling Flowers At The Lorimer Stop

This morning
I open the computer
gaze at the photograph

one half of your face
lost in darkness
the other
wanting release

Spring

March 21

Villa dei Misteri

You hand me a glass of wine walk across the floor and stand in front of a mirror and I realize I have never seen your reflection before and thought it might be a good idea to capture this moment learn a bit more about myself and how I got here so I sprint down the precariously narrow stairs of your apartment push open the door and run out to my car which I parked haphazardly because these days my eyesight tends to be blurred and I don't have the focus to even check if my car is the right distance from the curb then I remove my old camera from the trunk and still short of breath with heart racing from the descent down the rickety steps or from the vision of your reflection I blow the caked dust off the lens and recall the old postcard of an Italian village stuck haphazardly in your mirror between gold frame and glass and the reflection of your almond eyes flashing like mezzanotte marble reminded me of the winding road to Villa dei Misteri on the outskirts of Rome I traveled on years ago to see a fresco of a maenad her searching gaze deep and mysterious then with camera in hand still out of breath I ascend the narrow stairs and something in your apartment reminds me of a scene from an old Sophia Loren movie when my television was black and white Sophia in Rome at the bottom of the Spanish Steps her smokey eyes reveal something looming deep inside like how I feel when I look at you and am reminded of that winding road I traveled on to Villa dei Misteri when my driving skills were sharp and heart racing with excitement to see the fresco of the maenad and remember when Sophia turned her head and stared into the window of the empty cafe the director captures the reflection and I watched her narrowing eyes peering back at herself as the camera sealed the moment forever on celluloid intimacy that comes only when a woman looks at herself sees truth or a man standing behind her holding a glass of wine haphazardly in his hand looking not at her but the reflection revealing something lost like Sophia's complex eyes on a black and white screen

and you plunge the corkscrew into the bottle of Red Chianti gifted from me who parked haphazardly on your curb in the middle of the night in the pouring rain to leave something at the foot of your narrow steps not only to make you smile but to learn more about myself and how I got there in the first place then you gaze into the mirror and the end of the movie comes rushing back to me when the master director captures that moment that I had never seen before and like Sophia you turn your head slightly away from the lens and with lips closed and eyes narrowing you search the room for my empty wine glass resting haphazardly at the edge of your dresser amongst scattered bracelets hair pins and a ring and I look through the narrow eyepiece hold my breath and straighten my back then with the same precision and skill I used to navigate the winding road to Villa dei Misteri I gesture to you with my hand exactly where your eyes should rest to capture for the curious what surrounds me when I see you and why I ascend the precariously narrow stairs in the first place.

March 26

4 Syllables

While glancing at my early works
I came across the word tempestuous
realized I haven't used words
with 4 syllables or more
since the days before I met you
when I pretended to know myself
and walked the metaphysical higher ground
to fool others

April 2

Betrayal

Last night I packed away
my heavy white computer

worn keys with masking tape
holding the bubbled
rubber bottom in place

set my new feather light
razor thin shiny silver
laptop in front of my
waiting fingers

and submitted a new poem
to a sleek on-line magazine
called Instant Gratification

April 13

Vacations

Careening into my 60th year on the planet
I've come to realize
L   O   V   E
is the most difficult of all pursuits
to write about

so instead of thinking about it
I'll take vacations with that special person
walk barefoot on the beach
always with pen and paper close by
in case she turns to me
lays a hand on my cheek and says
let's go home

April 16

Electric Massager

This morning I attach
an electric massage apparatus

to the back of my chair
where I type these poems for you

heated metal balls kneading muscles
'round tangled spinal chords

with each deep rotation
the poem I outlined in my head

      breaks apart

free of pain I stare at a blank screen
unable to conjure any meaningful lines

so I grab my raincoat
stomp through puddles

remove boulders stuck in mud

hear a pop from ligaments tearing
pain creeping through dislocated vertebrate

when a vision lifts me from the earth
wipes dirt from my brow

with nerves still tense and firing
I limp back to my desk

bandages wrapped tight around my waist
and stitch together a heart-wrenching stanza

April 21

The Mechanics of Photography

This morning before a shoot, I
notice my recent portraits appear
flat, void of mystery, so

I walk through the mechanics,
focus on a bench with two lovers
press my nose to the plastic back

then feel a tug on my shoulder
you point to a magnolia tree
in full bloom, fragrance like lemon

and turn my lens to close-up, slide
your index finger over smooth metal hood
my body shuttering like the first time

May 1

The Cat

A creaking sound from the old wood floor outside my bedroom starts my mind racing as the large maine coon cat leaps from one stair to the platform of the other pushing open the half closed door with his head and I hear the sound of muffled paws landing gently on the persian carpet as he saunters to the far side of the bed where I sleep then finds his spot and sits in silence to check if I am reacting to his presence but my head is busy organizing a new chapter from our last conversation during our meeting to review progress of the outline for my latest book when you said to me maybe I should write this new novel in close first person to lay out for the world my real feelings not based on some story about an artist that can't find her true self so journeys to an unknown place way up north by a wide river with hawks and osprey and is so taken in by it all she regains inspiration and creates this masterwork and you said this feels forced lacking internal conflict you've admired in my work and remind me that this story has never really happened so the best I can hope for is a few moments when you lean over to check the manuscript and a lock of your hair tucked neatly behind your ear falls away slowly like an eagle in free fall swooping down on something moving

and clutches my forearm at the bone carrying me away to a cloudless sky

and together we circle above the house where my maine coon cat waits patiently for my return and I remember you said maybe I should write a novel based on how I feel when I am alone with you and from this unique vantage point with you gripping me I conjure up poetic verse with rich metaphors to express to the world in that cryptic way I have become so good at when no one except for me and maybe you knows who I am referring to then a gust of wind moves around us and you look over your shoulder at me with those sharp eyes focused on every movement of my mouth as I recite a few lines from this new work and you take me higher to gain more depth through a wider angle and I can look down and see everything even a woman sleeping soundly next to a large maine coon cat who has lost most of his natural instincts handed food that comes from a cannery in an old industrial town near a dark polluted river and I prop up the pillow and with blurry eyes look up at the ceiling and in this new chapter I am organizing in my head I watch another lock of your hair fall away from the other ear and brushes my arm like a single feather caressing an ancient spirit and I am so overwhelmed by this new sense of adventure that I shout through the prevailing winds to take me even higher and soar to a point where I can lose all perspective and my mind will reach some sort of bliss and be inspired to write this new story then suddenly without warning the air speed increases a howling gust breaks the silence then I feel your grip tightening and instinctively you glide into another air pocket for safety and I feel a piercing through my skin spreading over my trusting body creeping slowly inside through a half opened door then a sudden jolt of some kind of heavy turbulence bursting wide and landing on my groin with excited claws and I reach for your head and feel vibrations from a familiar purr and glance at the clock on the bedside table hoping it reads something like 7:36 but the red digital lines form the numbers 5:11 which is the same time the large maine coon cat wakes me every morning to commiserate that he too has had a long night and is hungry then leaps down positioning himself on the same spot on the persian carpet by the side of my bed meowing as he has done since the first time when he realized that this is all he needs to do when he is hungry so I dangle my hand near his head as a diversion to calm him in some way as I finish organizing the new chapter in my head but he is more playful than usual

and a claw
like a pin
pricks my finger

and feel blood so I lean over looking down at dilated orange pupils beaming at me in the still version of the breaking dawn

May 18

Rose

This morning
outside my window
orange and red light
lingers on the edge
of a cloud
yellow turns gold

set upon the desk
where I write these poems
for you, a rose
opens wider
than I've ever
seen before

maybe god exists
or just a muse tapping
have faith it says
chose a common noun
for the title
of this collection

one syllable
is all you'll need
then stand by it
be ready to defend
as the meaning
will change
and transform
over time

May 26

Too Much Emphasis on My Needs

The title of this poem
was conjured after
a self reflective moment
I had this morning
after reading my new works
and remembering why
self reflection is worthwhile
as long as you're selling books

June 3

The Monastery

Unable to finish
my latest poem
I return to the
Buddhist monastery

The meditation garden
in full bloom,
lilac and mint

My teacher says
to observe the natural order
draw her from memory,
shadows and lines
symmetry, proportion

Then without touching
my bald head
or wrinkled face,
explore the broken parts
draw a self portrait
through her eyes

Compare, be ready
to choose

Return and finish
the poem
or stay, observe
autumn colors
mist after rain
death in winter

June 7

A.D.D.

I wonder if it's a sin
to be inside her
thinking of the way
you looked yesterday

while handing me
my newspaper
wrapped in blue nylon
thrown by mistake
onto your stoop

morning light
on porcelain skin
hair in a loose
bun at the back
of your neck

and a summer dress
with tan stripes
like a Rodin subject
in celestial pose

pointing
to an article
about our
tech age

people having
difficulties
focusing,
even during sex

distracted easily
in the moment
like a short circuit
never present

thinking of
abstractions
like porcelain
and stripes
and the way
you wear your hair

June 10

Do Not Disturb

While eating eggs in a crowded cafe in Kingston, NY I watch you rub your eyes and remember how you struggle with allergies especially when we are out of the city causing your eyelids to swell and get itchy then turn red and offer to go to the car and get allergy pills and you grin that contemplative way I've grown used to and say to me

"it's not allergy season and why are you checking your cell phone during Sunday brunch?"

I remind you I'm my own boss and no one else will check on the weekends then you ask me to get more napkins to wipe your eyes so I walk over to the dark wood counter where steam rises from behind an espresso machine and a barista with fedora and snake tattoo twisting around a muscular arm looks at me from behind horn rimmed glasses

"how can I help you?" she says, pouring frothy milk into a tall slender glass and setting it on the counter in between two ceramic mugs made by a local artist

"these for sale?"

"only the blue one the red one is for display"

"can you put it in a box for me?"

and with my chest puffed out I return and say happy birthday lover and present you with a gift in a box but notice you are bent over close to my vibrating cell phone your eyelids red and swollen so I swipe at the keys set on the table and walk across the crowded lot to search the car for your pills

June 14

My Last Poem in a Series

Summer in the high sierras
rivers flow from melting lakes
light presses on granite

over time the earth
tilts away from the sun

mountain lakes freeze
craggy peaks erode

landslides like thunder
leave devastation in their wake

as when you turn the page
to arrive at my last poem
in a series

and recall your eyes
brushing over the words
like a hand on moss
after a storm

pressing on tender nerves
fingers resting longer
than usual

to discover I've moved aside
grabbed onto something sturdy

as I wait for the last rock to tumble
finding a clear path home

June 19

Blood Red Morning

the way a songbird
opens a blood red morning

a valentine card I place
at your gate

stepping cautiously
past the littered hydrant

I return to the solitude
of my parked car

humming the chorus
to the final stanza

my last line

the hypnotic glare
of your waking eyes

June 20

The Lines in Between

In the end
all I can hope for

is to arrive
with a drip more
insight

like summer rain
after a long drought

one by one

drops landing
on petals

a bud opens
thirsting for more

Paul Rabinowitz is an author, screenwriter, photographer, and founder of ARTS By The People. His works appear in *The Sun Magazine, New World Writing, Burningword, Evening Street Press, The Montreal Review,* and elsewhere. Rabinowitz was a featured artist in *Nailed Magazine* in 2020, *Mud Season Review* in 2022 and *Apricity Press* in 2023. He is the author of *The Clay Urn, Grand Street, Revisited, Confluence,* and *Limited Light,* a book of prose and portrait photography, which stems from his Limited Light photo series, nominated for Best of the Net in 2021. His poems and fiction are the inspiration for 8 award-winning experimental films, including Best Experimental Short at Cannes, Venice Shorts Film Festival, RevolutionME, Oregon Short Film Festival, Jersey Shore Film Festival and The Paris Film Festival. *truth, love and the lines in between* is his first full length book of poetry.

For more about Paul, visit his website: www.paulrabinowitz.com

www.ingramcontent.com/pod-product-compliance
Lightning Source LLC
Chambersburg PA
CBHW020340170426
43200CB00006B/447